I0417697

The Bible in Spain

[christmas summary classics]

(George Henry Borrow)

The Bible in Spain

I.—The First Journey

In 1835 George Henry Borrow, fresh from a journey in Russia as the Bible Society's agent, set out for Spain to sell and distribute Bibles on the Society's behalf. This mission, in the most fervidly Roman Catholic of all European countries, was one that required rare courage and resourcefulness; and Borrow's task was complicated by the fact that Spain was in a disturbed state owing to the Carlist insurrection. Borrow's journeys in Spain, which were preceded by a tour in Portugal, and followed by a visit to Morocco, lasted in all about four years. In December, 1842, he published "The Bible in Spain"—a work less remarkable as a record of missionary effort than as a vivid narrative of picturesque travel episodes, and a testimony to its author's keen delight in an adventurous life of wanderings in the open air.

I landed at Lisbon on November 12, 1835; and on January 5, 1836, I spurred down the hill of Elvas, on the Portuguese frontier, eager to arrive in old chivalrous romantic Spain. In little more than half an hour we arrived at a brook, whose waters ran vigorously between steep banks. A man who was standing on the side directed me to the ford in the squeaking dialect of Portugal; but whilst I was yet splashing through the water, a voice from the other bank hailed me, in the magnificent language of Spain, in this guise: "Charity, Sir Cavalier, for the love of God bestow an alms upon me, that I may purchase a mouthful of red wine!" In a moment I was on Spanish ground, and, having flung the beggar a small piece of silver, I cried in ecstasy: "Santiago y cierra España!" and scoured on my way with more speed than before.

I was now within half a league of Badajoz, where I spent the next three weeks. It was here that I first fell in with those singular people, the Zincali, Gitanos, or Spanish gypsies. My time was chiefly devoted to the gypsies, among whom, from long intercourse with various sections of their race in different parts of the world, I felt myself much more at home than with the silent, reserved men of Spain, with whom a foreigner might mingle for half a century without having half a dozen words addressed to him. So when the fierce gypsy, Antonio Lopez, offered to accompany me as guide on my journey towards Madrid, I accepted his offer. After a few days of travelling in his company I was nearly arrested on suspicion by a national guard, but was saved by my passport. In fact, my appearance was by no means calculated to prepossess people in my favour. Upon my head I wore an old Andalusian hat; a rusty cloak, which had perhaps served half a dozen generations, enwrapped my body. My face was plentifully bespattered with mud, and upon my chin was a beard of a week's growth.

I took leave of Antonio at the summit of the Pass of Mirabete, and descended alone, occasionally admiring one of the finest prospects in the world; before me outstretched lay immense plains, bounded in the distance by huge mountains, whilst at the foot of the hill rolled the Tagus in a deep narrow stream, between lofty banks.

Early in February I reached Madrid. I hoped to obtain permission from the government to print the new Testament in the Castilian language, for circulation in Spain, and lost no time in seeing Mendizabal, the Prime Minister. He was a bitter enemy to the Bible Society; but I pressed upon him so successfully that eventually I obtained a promise that at the expiration of a few months, when he hoped the country would be in a more tranquil state, I should be allowed to print the Scriptures. He told me to call upon him again at the end of three months. Before that time had elapsed, however, he had fallen into disgrace, and his Ministry had been succeeded by another. At the outset, in spite of assistance from the British Minister, I could only get evasions from the new government.

I had nothing to do but wait, and I used to loiter for hours along the delightful banks of the canal that runs parallel with the River Manzanares, listening to the prattle of the narangero, or man who sold oranges and water. He was a fellow of infinite drollery; his knowledge of individuals was curious and extensive, few people passing his stall with whose names, character, and history he was not acquainted.

"Those two boys are the children of Gabiria, comptroller of the Queen's household, and the richest man in Madrid. They are nice boys, and buy much fruit. The old woman who is lying beneath yon tree is the Tia Lucilla; she has committed murders, and as she owes me money, I hope one day to see her executed. This man was of the Walloon guard—Señor Don Benito Mol, how do you do?"

This last-named personage instantly engrossed my attention; he was a bulky old man, with ruddy features, and eyes that had an expression of great eagerness, as if he were expecting the communication of some important tidings. He returned the salutation of the orange-man, and, bowing to me, forthwith produced two scented wash-balls, which he offered for sale in a rough dissonant jargon.

Upon my asking him who he was, the following conversation ensued between us.

"I am a Swiss of Lucerne, Benedict Mol by name, once a soldier in the Walloon guard, and now a soap-boiler, at your service."

"You speak the language of Spain very imperfectly," said I. "How long have you been in the country?"

"Forty-five years," replied Benedict. "But when the guard was broken up I went to Minorca, where I lost the Spanish language without acquiring the Catalan. I will now speak Swiss to you, for, if I am not much mistaken, you are a German man, and understand the speech of Lucerne. I intend shortly to return to Lucerne, and live there like a duke."

"Have you, then, realised a large capital in Spain?" said I, glancing at his hat and the rest of his apparel.

"Not a cuart, not a cuart; these two wash-balls are all that I possess."

"Perhaps you are the son of good parents, and have lands and money in your own country wherewith to support yourself?"

"Not a heller, not a heller; my father was hangman of Lucerne, and when he died his body was seized to pay his debts." When he went back to Lucerne, added Benedict, it would be in a coach drawn by six mules, with treasure, a mighty schatz, which lay in a certain church at Compostella, in Galicia. He had learnt the secret of it from a dying soldier of the Walloon guard, who, with two companions, had buried in the church a great booty they had made in Portugal. It consisted of gold moidores and of a packet of huge diamonds from the Brazils. The whole was contained in a large copper kettle. "It is very easy to find, for the dying man was so exact in his description of the place where it lies that were I once at Compostella, I should have no difficulty in putting my hand upon it. Several times I have been on the point of setting out on the journey, but something has always happened to stop me."

At various times during the next two years I again met Benedict Mol.

When next I called upon the new Prime Minister, Isturitz, I found him well disposed to favour my views, and I obtained an understanding that my Biblical pursuits would be tolerated in Spain. The Minister was in a state of extreme depression, which was indeed well grounded; for within a week there occurred a revolution in which his party, the Moderados, were overthrown by the Nacionals. I watched the fighting from an upper window, in the company of my friend D——, of the "Morning Chronicle." Afterwards I returned to England, for the purpose of consulting with my friends, and planning a Biblical campaign.

II.—*Travels in Northern Spain*

In November I sailed from the Thames to Cadiz, and reached Madrid by Seville and Cordova. I found that I could commence printing the Scriptures without any further applications to the government. Within three months of my arrival an edition of the New Testament, consisting of 5,000 copies, was published at Madrid. I then prepared to ride forth, Testament in hand, and endeavour to circulate the Word of God amongst the Spaniards.

First, I purchased a horse. He was a black Andalusian stallion of great power and strength, but he was unbroke, savage, and furious. A cargo of Bibles, however, which I hoped occasionally to put on his back, would, I had no doubt, thoroughly tame him. I then engaged a servant, a wandering Greek, named Antonio Buchini; his behaviour was frequently in the highest degree extraordinary, but he served me courageously and faithfully.

The state of the surrounding country was not very favourable for setting forth; Cabrera, the Carlist, was within nine leagues of Madrid, with an army nearly 10,000 strong; nevertheless, about the middle of May I bade farewell to my friends, and set out for Salamanca.

A melancholy town is Salamanca; the days of its collegiate glory are long since past, never more to return; a circumstance, however, which is little to be regretted, for what benefit did the world ever derive from scholastic philosophy? The principal bookseller of the town consented to become my agent here, and I, in consequence, deposited in his shop a certain number of New Testaments. I repeated this experiment in all the large towns which I visited and distributed them likewise as I rode along.

The posada where I put up at Salamanca was a good specimen of the old Spanish inn. Opposite to my room lodged a wounded officer; he was attended by three broken soldiers, lame or maimed, and unfit for service; they were quite destitute of money, and the officer himself was poor and had only a few dollars. Brave guests for an inn, thought I; yet, to the honour of Spain be it spoken, it is one of the few countries in Europe where poverty is never insulted nor looked upon with contempt. Even at an inn the poor man is never spurned from the door, and if not harboured, is at least dismissed with fair words, and consigned to the mercy of God and his mother. This is as it should be. I laugh at the bigotry and prejudices of Spain; I abhor the cruelty and ferocity which have cast a stain of eternal infamy on her history; but I will say for the Spaniards that in their social intercourse no people in the world exhibit a juster feeling of what is due to the dignity of human nature, or better understand the behaviour which it behoves a man to adopt towards his fellow beings.

We travelled on by Valladolid, Leon and Astorga, and entered the terrific mountains of Galicia. After a most difficult journey, along precipitous tracks that were reported to be infested by brigands, we reached Coruña, where stands the tomb of Mocre, built by the chivalrous French in commemoration of the fall of their heroic antagonist. Many acquire immortality without seeking it, and die before its first ray has gilded their name; of these was Moore. There is scarcely a Spaniard but has heard of his tomb, and speaks of it with a strange kind of awe.

At the commencement of August I found myself at St. James of Compostella. A beautiful town is St. James, standing on a pleasant level amidst mountains. Time has been when, with the single exception of Rome, it was the most celebrated resort of pilgrims in the world. Its glory, however, as a place of pilgrimage is rapidly passing away.

I was walking late one night alone in the Alameda, when a man dressed in coarse brown garments took off his hat and demanded charity in uncouth tones. "Benedict Mol," said I, "is it possible that I see you at Compostella?"

It was indeed Benedict. He had walked all the way from Madrid, supporting himself by begging.

"What motive could possibly bring you such a distance?" I asked him.

"I come for the schatz—the treasure. Ow, I do not like this country of Galicia at all; all my bones are sore since I entered Galicia."

"And yet you have come to this country in search of treasure?"

"Ow yaw, but the schatz is buried; it is not above ground; there is no money above ground in Galicia. I must dig it up; and when I have dug it up I will purchase a coach with six mules, and ride out of Galicia to Lucerne."

I gave him a dollar, and told him that as for the treasure he had come to seek, probably it only existed in his own imagination.

III.—The Alcalde of Finisterra

After a visit to Pontevedra and Vigo, I returned to Padron, three leagues from Compostella, and decided to hire a guide to Cape Finisterra. It would be difficult to assign any plausible reason for the ardent desire which I entertained to visit this place; but I thought that to convey the Gospel to a place so wild and remote might perhaps be considered an acceptable pilgrimage in the eyes of my Maker.

The first guide I employed deserted me; the second did not appear to know the way, and sought to escape from me; and when I tried to pursue him, my horse bolted and nearly broke my neck. I caught the guide at last. After a very rough journey we reached the village of Finisterra, and wound our way up the flinty sides of the huge bluff head which is called the Cape. Certainly in the whole world there is no bolder coast than the Gallegan shore. There is an air of stern and savage grandeur in everything around, which strangely captivates the imagination. After gazing from the summit of the Cape for nearly an hour we descended to the village. On reaching the house where we had taken up our habitation, I flung myself on a rude and dirty bed, and was soon asleep.

I was suddenly, however, seized roughly by the shoulder and nearly dragged from the bed. I looked up in amazement, and I beheld hanging over me a wild and uncouth figure; it was that of an elderly man, built as strong as a giant, in the habiliments of a fisherman; in his hand was a rusty musket.

Myself: Who are you and what do you want? By what authority do you thus presume to interfere with me?

Figure: By the authority of the Justicia of Finisterra. Follow me peaceably, Calros, or it will be the worse with you.

"Calros," said I, "what does the person mean?" I thought it, however, most prudent to obey his command, and followed him down the staircase. The shop and the portal were now thronged with the inhabitants of Finisterra, men, women, and children. Through this crowd the figure pushed his way with an air of authority. "It is Calros! It is Calros!" said a hundred voices; "he has come to Finisterra at last, and the justicia have now got hold of him."

At last we reached a house of rather larger size than the rest; my guide having led me into a long, low room, placed me in the middle of the floor, and then hurrying to the door, he endeavoured to repulse the crowd who strove to enter with us. I now looked around the room. It was rather scantily furnished; I could see nothing but some tubs and barrels, the mast of a boat, and a sail or two. Seated upon the tubs were three or four men coarsely dressed, like fishermen or shipwrights. The principal personage was a surly, ill-tempered-looking fellow of about thirty-five, whom I discovered to be the alcalde of Finisterra. After I had looked about me for a minute, the alcalde, giving his whiskers a twist, thus addressed me:

"Who are you, where is your passport, and what brings you to Finisterra?"

Myself: I am an Englishman. Here is my passport, and I came to see Finisterra.

This reply seemed to discomfit them for a moment. They looked at each other, then at my passport. At length the alcalde, striking it with his finger, bellowed forth, "This is no Spanish passport; it appears to be written in French."

Myself: I have already told you that I am a foreigner. I, of course, carry a foreign passport.

Alcalde: Then you mean to assert that you are not Calros Rey?

Myself: I never heard before of such a king, nor indeed of such a name.

Alcalde: Hark to the fellow; he has the audacity to say that he has never heard of Calros the pretender, who calls himself king.

Myself: If you mean by Calros the pretender Don Carlos, all I can reply is that you can scarcely be serious. You might as well assert that yonder poor fellow, my guide, whom I see you have made prisoner, is his nephew, the infante Don Sebastian.

Alcalde: See, you have betrayed yourself; that is the very person we suppose him to be.

Myself: It is true that they are both hunchbacks. But how can I be like Don

Carlos? I have nothing the appearance of a Spaniard, and am nearly a foot taller than the pretender.

Alcalde: That makes no difference; you, of course, carry many waistcoats about you, by means of which you disguise yourself, and appear tall or low according to your pleasure.

This last was so conclusive an argument that I had of course nothing to reply to it. "Yes, it is Calros; it is Calros," said the crowd at the door.

"It will be as well to have these men shot instantly," continued the alcalde; " if they are not the two pretenders, they are at any rate two of the factious."

"I am by no means certain that they are either one or the other," said a gruff voice. Our glances rested upon the figure who held watch at the door. He had planted the barrel of his musket on the floor, and was leaning his chin against the butt.

"I have been examining this man," he continued, pointing to myself, "and listening whilst he spoke, and it appears to me that after all he may prove an Englishman; he has their very look and voice."

Here the alcalde became violently incensed. "He is no more an Englishman than yourself," he exclaimed; "if he were an Englishman, would he have come in this manner, skulking across the land? Not so I trow. He would have come in a ship."

After a fierce dispute between the alcalde and the guard, it was decided to remove us to Corcuvion, where the head alcalde was to dispose of us as he thought proper.

The head alcalde was a mighty liberal and a worshipper of Jeremy Bentham. "The most universal genius which the world ever produced," he called him. "I am most truly glad to see a countryman of his in these

Gothic wildernesses. Stay, I think I see a book in your hand."

Myself: The New Testament.

Alcalde: Why do you carry such a book with you?

Myself: One of my principal motives in visiting Finisterra was to carry this book to that wild place.

Alcalde: Ah, ah! how very singular. Yes, I remember. I have heard that the English highly prize this eccentric book. How very singular that the countrymen of the grand Bentham should set any value upon that old monkish book.

I told him that I had read none of Bentham's writings; but nevertheless I had to thank that philosopher not only for my release, but for hospitable treatment during the rest of my stay in the region of Finisterra.

From Corcuvion I returned to Compostella and Coruña, and then directed my course to Asturias. At Oviedo, I again met Benedict Mol. He had sought to get permission to disinter the treasure, and had not succeeded. He had then tried to reach France, begging by the way. He was in villainous apparel, and nearly barefooted. He promised to quit Spain and return to Lucerne, and I gave him a few dollars.

"A strange man is this Benedict," said my servant Antonio. "A strange life he has led and a strange death he will die—it is written on his countenance. That he will leave Spain I do not believe, or, if he leave it, itwill only be to return, for he is bewitched about this same treasure."

Soon afterwards I returned to Madrid. During my northern journey, which occupied a considerable portion of the year 1837, I had accomplished less than I proposed to myself. Something, however, had been effected. The

New Testament was now enjoying a quiet sale in the principal towns of the north.

I had, moreover, disposed of a considerable number of Testaments with my own hands.

IV.—The Persecution

I spent some months in Madrid translating the New Testament into the Basque and Gypsy languages. During this time the hostility of the priesthood to my labours became very bitter. The Governor of Madrid forbade the sale of Testaments in January, 1838; afterwards all copies of the Gypsy Gospel were confiscated, and in May I was thrown into prison. I went cheerfully enough, knowing that the British Embassy was actively working for my release; and the governor of the prison, one of the greatest rascals in all Spain, greeted me with a most courteous speech in pure sonorous Castilian, bidding me consider myself as a guest rather than a prisoner, and permitting me to roam over every part of the gaol.

What most surprised me with respect to the prisoners was their good behaviour. I call it good when all things are taken into consideration. They had their occasional bursts of wild gaiety, their occasional quarrels, which they were in the habit of settling in a corner with their long knives; but, upon the whole, their conduct was infinitely superior to what might have been expected. Yet this was not the result of coercion, or any particular care which was exercised over them; for perhaps in no part of the world are prisoners so left to themselves and so utterly neglected as in Spain. Yet in this prison of Madrid the ears of the visitor are never shocked with horrid blasphemy and profanity, nor are his eyes outraged and himself insulted. And yet in this prison were some of the most desperate characters in Spain. But gravity and sedateness are the leading characteristics of the Spaniards, and the very robber, except in those moments when he is engaged in his occupation, and then no one is more sanguinary, pitiless, and wolfishly eager for booty, is a being who can be courteous and affable, and who takes pleasure in conducting himself with sobriety and decorum.

After a stay of three weeks in the prison I was released, as I expected, with an apology, and I prepared for another journey. While in prison I had been visited by Benedict Mol, again in Madrid. Soon after my release he came in high spirits to bid me farewell before starting for Compostella to dig up the schatz. He was dressed in new clothes; instead of the ragged staff he had usually borne, he carried a huge bamboo rattan. He had endured terrible privations, he said, in the mountains. But one night he had heard among the rocks a mysterious voice telling him that the way to the treasure lay through Madrid. To Madrid he had come, and the government, hoping for a replenishment of its empty treasury, had given him permission to search for the treasure.

"Well, Benedict," I told him, "I have nothing to say save that I hope you will succeed in your digging."

"Thank you, lieber Herr, thank you!" Here he stopped short and started. "Heiliger Gott!

Suppose I should not find the treasure, after all?"

"Very rationally said. It is not too late. Put on your old garments, grasp your ragged staff, and help me to circulate the Gospel."

He mused for a moment, then shook his head. "No,no," he cried; "I must accomplish my destiny! I shall find it—the schatz—it is still there—it *must* be there!"

He went, and I never saw him more. What I heard, however, was extraordinary enough. The treasure hunt at Compostella was conducted in a public and imposing manner. The bells pealed, the populace thronged from their houses, troops were drawn up in the square. A procession directed its course to the church; at its head was the captain-general and the Swiss; numerous masons brought up the rear. The procession enters the church, they pass through it in solemn march, they find themselves in a vaulted passage. The Swiss looks around. "Dig here!" said he. The masons labour, the floor is broken up—a horrible fetid odour arises....

Enough; no treasure was found, and the unfortunate Swiss was forthwith seized and flung into the horrid prison of Saint James, amidst the execrations of thousands. Soon afterwards he was removed from Saint James, whither I could not ascertain. It was said that he disappeared on the road.

Where in the whole cycle of romance shall we find anything more wild, grotesque and sad than the easily authenticated history of the treasure-digger of Saint James.

A most successful journey, in which I distributed the Gospel freely in the Sagra of Toledo and La Mancha, was interrupted by a serious illness, which compelled me to return to Madrid, and afterwards to visit England for a rest. On December 31, 1838, I entered Spain for the third time. From Cadiz I travelled to

Madrid by Seville, and made a number of short journeys to the villages near the capital. The clergy, however, had induced the government to order the confiscation of all Testaments exposed for sale. Prevented from labouring in the villages, I organised a distribution of Testaments in Madrid itself. I then returned to Seville; but even here I was troubled by the government's ordersfor the seizure of Testaments. I had, however, several hundred copies in my own possession, and I remained in Seville for several months until I had disposed of them. I lived there in extreme retirement; there was nothing to induce me to enter much into society. The Andalusians, in all estimable traits of character, are as far below the other Spaniards as the country which they inhabit is superior in beauty and fertility to the other provinces of Spain.

At the end of July, 1839, I went by steamer down the Guadalquivir to Cadiz, then to Gibraltar, and thence across to Tangier and the land of the Moors. I had a few Spanish Testaments still in my possession, and my object was to circulate them among the Christians of Tangier.

Note.—At this point the narrative abruptly ends. Borrow returned from Morocco to England in the spring of 1840.

The End

www.ingramcontent.com/pod-product-compliance
Lightning Source LLC
Chambersburg PA
CBHW070257300526
45791CB00022B/1612